AF255918

NATIVE AMERICAN HERBALISM BIBLE 1

By

ROSEMARY KENNEDY

loss due to the information herein, either directly or indirectly.

Respective authors own all copyrights not held by the publisher.

The information herein is offered for informational purposes solely and is universal as such. The presentation of the information is without a contract or any type of guarantee assurance.

The trademarks used are without any consent, and the publication of the trademark is without permission or backing by the trademark owner. All trademarks and brands within this book are for clarifying purposes only and are owned by the owners themselves, not affiliated with this document.

Table of Contents

Introduction 1

Chapter 1: History of Herbalism....................................**4**

1.1 Herbal Medicine's Role in Different Cultures 5

1.2 Application, Positive Effect & Active Medicinal Components 10

1.3 Control, Legislation, Awareness and Regulation on Use 10

Chapter 2: Powerful Herbs...**16**

2.1. The Most Powerful Herbs...16

Chapter 3: Herbal Encyclopedia **25**

3.1. Herb's Encyclopedia...25

Chapter 4: Handling of the Herbs **40**

4.1. Postharvest Handling of Herbs................................40

Chapter 5: Herbs and Modern Medicines.......................**49**

5.1 Native American Herbs and Modern Health Supplements 49

5.2. Native American's medical system 57

Conclusion **59**

INTRODUCTION

Traditional herbal medicines possess a substantial use historically, and this is true even today, as many herbal products are available in the market these days. In developing countries, major populations rely on conventional herbal practitioners to meet their healthcare needs. Although this is the age of modern medicines, herbal medicines have maintained their importance and popularity in every decade of life due to significant cultural reasons. In some countries, herbal medicines are subjected to manufacturing standards but not everywhere. For example, Germany sells herbal medicines as "phytomedicines," as manufacturers follow some safety and quality standards. In the USA, mostly herbal medicines are available as dietary supplements in the marketplace. Many diseases have been treated pharmacologically using herbal medicines.

Development and the mass production of chemical drugs have revolutionized social health care systems in modern developed countries. However, in many developing countries, a large population relies upon traditional medication methods for primary care. For example, according to some statistical data, 90% population in Africa and 70 % population in India depend upon conventional medications for healthcare requirements. According to World Health Organization – 2005, 90% of general hospitals have special units for traditional medicines in China.

For the past two decades, the public's interest has developed, especially in traditional natural therapies for their basic healthcare. It is not limited to just under developing countries because of its long-lasting encouraging outcomes. General stats show that 12% of children in the US and 38% of adults used traditional herbal medicines in 2007. According to a survey conducted by National Center, the use of herbal therapy or natural products besides minerals & vitamins was 18.8%. According to data collected in a survey conducted in 2003 in Hong Kong, 40% population showed their interest in natural herbal treatment than western manufactured medicines through a chemical process. In a survey conducted in the United States, 12.8% of 21.923 young adults used herbal supplements at least once in their life. In a second survey, almost 42% of the population used dietary supplements and minerals and multivitamins, followed by garlic, Ginkgo, flax, and palmetto.

Generally, people use herbal medicines as affordable and more satisfactory in terms of patients' ideology and free from adverse side effects, unlike chemically synthesized medicines. Most herbal medicines are used in chronic treatments and health promotion as opposed to life-threatening situations. However, the use of allopathic medicines increases where the herbal or conventional medicines become ineffective, for example, cancer, several infectious diseases and allergies.

CHAPTER 1:
HISTORY OF HERBALISM

Herbal medicines are generally accepted as non-toxic and safe alternatives to chemical medicines. Herbal medicine is now a globally flourishing commercial enterprise. Most people worldwide perceive the natural world as sacred. Access to healthcare facilities is not easy; medical expenses are increasing with each passing day. The middle-class population suffers a lot and is refused to access high-quality health care. For them, herbal medicines are the best and satisfactory solution.

1.1 Herbal Medicine's Role in Different Cultures

The use of herbs in pharmacological treatment was started a long time ago. Folk healing methods using herbs generally were used all over the world as their culture and tradition. Some of those traditions are described briefly in the following sections and some examples of healing practices with herbs.

Traditional Medicines in China

Since ancient times, traditional medicines have been used by the Chines people. Although the mineral and animal extracts were being used fundamental source for remedies was botanical. 500 out of 12000 herbal items are in common use. These botanical items can be used after some general processing techniques, including stir, frying, soak in vinegar/wine. Traditional remedies are often used after some prescription or individualized methodology in clinical practice.

These traditional herbal remedies are still in common use in China; more than 50% population uses these herbal items at least once a day, daily commonly; in rural areas, the prevalence rate of herbal items is much higher than in urban areas. Almost 5000 herbal remedies are generally available in China, and they contribute almost 1/5th of the entire pharmaceutical market of China.

Traditional Medicines in Japan

Numerous herbal remedies after China have become popular in Japan as well. In the 9th Century Herbs, natives were categorized as the 1st pharmacopeia of traditional medicines in Japan.

Traditional Medicines in India

For 500 years, Ayurveda herbal medical systems have been practicing in India. It included not only the medicines but dietary remedies as well. They emphasize the mind, body, and spiritual power and herbal remedies in healing and treatment.

Herbal Medicines in Europe, the USA, and other Countries

North America and Europe have incorporated the traditional herbal healing remedies in their complementary, alternative, and holistic, or we may say that integrative health care medical system. In the late 20th century, the growing public interest in self-care resulted in massive growth in traditional herbal healing modalities, especially in the USA. Users have responded with positive remarks towards these herbal remedies because they thought they were safe, feasible, effective, and economical than synthetic chemical items. They take them as part of a healthy lifestyle, and they thought that these herbal medicines could keep them safe from the harmful effects of chemically synthesized medical items.

After centuries of positive and healthy outcomes herbal, medicines are now vigorously incorporated with modern medical practices to replace the synthetic version of the medicine. Ingredients that have been used in herbal healing systems are now used in modern developed countries as an essential part of disease prevention and health promotion, thus replacing acute treatment with chronic exposure. Herbal products are used for weight loss purposes. It doesn't mean that modern medicines are not safe. Still, the meaning of the whole discussion is that herbal medicines are comparatively better in results with long-lasting health effects, and generally prescribed as safer options in public.

Individualization of herbal prescriptions is the major issue for translating traditional herbal remedies to conventional western medicine. For massive market production of herbal medicines, one of the main issues is standardization, which lacks due to the few traditional herbalists, or we may say that a person working on herbal medicine on a small scale standardization means understanding the conditions for growth, harvesting time, extraction strategy and other material for preparation with an active ingredient provision public. But for the larger distributors doing business in supermarkets or working with different authorized companies' standardization means to work under defined and pre-set conditions for well manufacturing practices.

In the USA, both the large and small, scale manufacturers of herbal medicines are working with a wide range of variations in quality and efficacy in the marketplace. However, all dietary herbal supplement producers do not require adherence to standardized manufacturing practices in the USA. That is why quality is not assured yet. This mostly public in the USA is discouraged by herbal products casual use, because of the shocking revelations about consistent ingredients missing in the products or the claimed or labeled quantity of ingredients.

For the common use of herbal products, the efficacy may be commonly based upon testimonials, traditional use and both uncontrolled & controlled studies because of their increasingly common use and recommendations. Questions about the safety concerns for some of the herbal ingredients have been raised because of some adverse outcomes, related to their common use increasingly due to the clinically relevant demonstrative interactions between prescribed drugs and some herbs.

Many adverse events like heart attack, stroke, seizures, liver toxicity, and irregularities in heart rate, deaths and psychoses are related to the excess use of ephedra for weight loss or increased energy. Bodybuilding purposes widely used in Canada and increasingly in Europe to deal with nervousness, pain, muscle tension, anxiety have caused some countries to ban these products. Due to the common use, few herbs have been found to cause cancer, for example, Rubies, Maringa, Aristo lochia and Senecio Riddellii. It does not mean that these herbs are banned, but the use of these herbs is now regularized with some special purposes.

Herbal Medicines in the Developed Countries

There is a long history of using plants & their metabolite constituents in modern (western) medicine and some traditional medical systems. They are the source of some vital important famous drugs like Codeine, Morphine, Atropine, Digoxin, and Vincristine. In developed countries, the utilization of herbal medicines has now widely expanded since the mid-half of the 20th century. Monographs of certain selected herbs are easily accessible from various sources. For example, the ESCOP (European Scientific Cooperation On Phototherapy), WHO (World Health Organization) and German Commission E.

Monographs by WHO explain the herbs in numbers of criteria, including their vernacular names and synonyms, commonly used parts of herbs, geographical distribution, identification and characterization tests with micro & macroscopic examination purity test, dosing, their active principles, and their adverse reactions. Other herbal information sources give details about the herbal products currently used, such as a comprehensive database by Natural

Medicines & Napralert, which provides info. About available databases about herbal remedies and items.

1.2 Application, Positive Effect & Active Medicinal Components

In some special situations, the active principles for herbal-derived products are characterized and isolated to understand their action mechanisms, for example, ephedrine alkaloids in certain species of the Ephedra. For most of the herbal items, this kind of information is missing or incomplete, which is of no use. The reason behind this is the complexity lying in botanical preparations and structure. It is the most common and well-accepted aspect by the public that active principles of herbal preparations are responsible for their healthy and beneficial effects.

1.3 Control, Legislation, Awareness and Regulation on Use

WHO instructions for herbal remedies

A group of experts was invited by the regional office of "WHO" in 1992, to formulate the principles and criteria development for research and evaluation of herbal medicines. The importance of herbal products was recognized in this meeting to view its' widely spread use, efficacy and increasing demand. Some herbal medicines are regulated through scientific testing, but many others are used just because of traditional reasons to restore, improve, and protect health. Still, numerous herbal medicines are widely available in the marketplace, which must be studied thoroughly despite their vast use over the decades with encouraging outcomes. Although herbal medicines are being used with a wide acceptance rate, there is still a gap in satisfactory research about their efficacy and safety is missing.

Assessment guidelines for herbal medicines are composed by "WHO" in 1996. These guidelines are about the criteria for quality assurance, efficacy, and safety to assist the regulatory authorities, assisting the producers in documentation and submissions regarding these products. The basic purpose behind this was to make sure the long-term beneficial use of such medicines. Under these guidelines, the regulatory authorities were given the authority to cancel the license of registered producers because of certain toxic effects of herbal medicines.

Herbal medicines vary from country to country in terms of importance. These products are not available as a homogenous group but are completely licensed and registered medicinal products with proven efficacy and safety standards, after several clinical trials and published literature.

EU Definition of Herbal Products

In council directives by EU implemented as national law in all the member states, it has mentioned that a pre-marketing approval is compulsory for any herbal product before launching on the public level. A proper definition for herbal medicine is available in terms of safety, compositions, plants, and efficacy necessary to be fulfilled by any manufacturer.

Classification of Traditional Herbal Products

Herbal products are considered medicinal items if they indicate therapeutic or prophylactic and do not come under the category of medicine if these indications are not present. Most products are not categorized as medicinal items; although they show some pharmacological properties still, they are only used in cosmetic and food areas. For example, the Senna seeds of the Cassia plant are used as laxatives. In Spain, UK and Ireland, certain preparations exist, defined as medicinal items under specific conditions exempted from the licensing requirements.

Combination Products

Ingredients are used in combination generally in Europe, and assessment is done under some specific guidelines. A combination of homeopathic and herbal products is used in some countries. Their assessment is done under strict criteria. Vitamins and herbal ingredients are used in combination in various countries.

Quality, Safety & Efficacy

In all European member states, authorization and quality assurance according to the given guidelines is mandatory. There is the exception that herbal product data can be published with some references in Denmark and Finland. The bibliographical choice is sometimes provided through the assessment but practically not used. In Austria, for safe documentation, such kind of application is permitted.

Simple Proof of Efficacy

Licensed herbal products are available in many EU member states. National authorities are responsible for ensuring their quality and safety. A long-term simplified experimental protocol is necessary to ensure the efficacy of herbal products. For example, Austria, France, Belgium and Germany are strictly followed by the authorities. However, there are other EU member states as well who do not follow this strategy.

<u>*Developed Products*</u>

Herbal products specified for non-traditional modified (highly processed or extracted especially) fully licensed authorization are required. It is necessary to prove the efficacy of the product through clinical trials.

<u>*Individual Supply*</u>

1 to 1 consultation is made up between practitioner and patient to maintain the successful supply chain of herbal products. An approved formula is used to manufacture herbal medicine by pharmacists. According to section 12 in the UK of Medicine Act 1968, no authorization is required if the medicine is manufactured under specified conditions.

<u>*Foreign Products*</u>

Methods of quality assurances for medicinal plants and their manufacturing strategy are different in member states. For some specific situations, there are no regulations, for example, raw materials controlling and crude drugs, etc.; especially those products that enter the market as foodstuff. But newly entered products with special finishing require efficacy, quality, and safety assurance.

<u>*Quality Control & Manufacturing Practices*</u>

All the member states are responsible for fulfilling the manufacturing requirements under section 75/319/EEC for herbal products. European Pharmacopeia controls the starting constituents for herbal products in all member states. Manufacturing processes are inspected in all the member states.

Surveillance for Post-marketing

Authorized herbal medical products are monitored in all the member states through a proper reaction reporting system. This system has shown its effectiveness with the withdrawal of several medically authorized products due to their safety concerns. The acceptance trend for such reports varies between the member states.

CHAPTER 2: POWERFUL HERBS

2.1. The Most Powerful Herbs

Most research on herbs is done in the areas where the consumption of herbal items comes in the mainstream, especially in Europe and Asia. Since the last three decades, the health authority in Germany has reviewed almost 200 herbs and composed effective clinical guidelines. The number of patients using different herbs or seek prescriptions from physicians for medical purposes is increasing. 1/3rd of the American population believes in the use of herbs for healthcare purposes. However, sometimes, people lag in quality information about herbal remedies' efficacy, quality, and safety. Considering the increasing demand for herbal products, well-defined quality data is mandatory for the patients and physicians. Here is a brief description of the herbs commonly used herbs in America for medical and healthcare purposes:

Chamomile

It is a powerful antioxidant. Chamomile is like an apple-scented herbal flower being used for thousands of years for medical purposes. Anglo Saxons said that Chamomile is one of the nine sacred herbs given by God to humans. It is taken as "Cure-all" in contemporary Germany. It is cultivated all over the world for anti-filamentary, vulnerary, spasmolytic and soothing purposes. The researchers have evaluated the traditional uses of this herb.

Vulnerary effects of chamomile in different controlled studies have been studied with neutral results. In a study (164 patients) by RDBPC, no significant difference was observed between experimental and placebo groups to prevent mucositis. However, researchers believed that the study was too short of reaching any certain conclusion as mucositis is caused due to immunosuppression. In a randomized controlled study, the reactions of Chamomile on a skin affected by radiation reactions, the results were not statistically significant.

Animal trial studies supported the use of chamomiles as a strong anti-inflammatory and antioxidant agent. It is also useful for gastric ulcers caused by medicinal reactions, alcohol, and stress.

Chamomile is also safe to use during pregnancy or childhood. It's therapeutic and safety effects have been found satisfactorily effective in several human trials. Significantly encouraging safety results of chamomile in several control studies make it safe to use as a home remedy for skin allergies; irritations agitate nerves and cramps. In the US, it is used as a tea and applied as a compress. However, while taking chamomile, there is a precaution not to be taken with any other sedatives like alcohol or "zodiazapines."

Echinacea

It is like a purple coneflower. It is used as an anticancer and for the treatment of wounds and colds. But it may cause immunity suppression with casual excess use. Mostly found in North America. But with the induction of antibiotics in the market, their popularity decreased but still a useful popular herb in the United States, generating 300 million dollars. 3 of 9 species of Echinacea are abundantly used for medical purposes. FDA in Germany has approved it for the treatment of infections in the upper respiratory tract, urogenital allergy, and severe wounds. In the USA, Echinacea alone or combined with other herbs is used as a booster for the human immune system. 26 controlled studies have proved the satisfactory positive results of Echinacea to be used as a home remedy. Two RDBPC trial studies have shown statistically healthy results in the experiment of using Echinacea as a medicinal item for the treatment of respiratory infection.

Feverfew

This herb is commonly used to treat the migraine and as an anti-arthritic. Its side effects include oral ulcers, headaches, and rare allergic reactions. It is a commonly found herb in gardens and roadsides. In a trial study, Feverfew has been found to reduce the migraine frequency up to 70%. Health officials in Canada have recently approved the Feverfew to treat headaches in encapsulated form, based on positive outcomes in several controlled studies. In different experimental studies, Feverfew has been found to reduce allergic inflammations.

Garlic

Garlic has been used for a wide range of medical purposes worldwide, due to which it has become the most studied herb. Various epidemiological and animal studies successfully prove it an anticancer agent and an anti-atherosclerotic agent as well. Meta-analysis of RPC trials shows that garlic has the cholesterol-lowering capability and, thus, performs a key role against obesity and effective for people suffering from hyperlipidemia. Within one month of onset treatment, a considerable decrease in weight can be observed by the person; thus, benefits of using garlic as an anti-lipidemic agent are inevitable. For people who suffer from high BP issues due to obesity or hyperlipidemia, garlic is a cure for this issue. Various controlled studies have shown satisfactory positive results of using garlic to treat hypertension. It is useful for high cholesterol patients to take garlic as it is safe to use, effective, and inexpensive.

Ginger

For thousands of years, ginger has been used as a powerful medicinal and culinary herb by practitioners and herbal physicians. Chinese have been using this for more than 2500 years as an antiemetic and flavoring agent. Greeks in ancient times used to wrap the chunks of ginger in reading and eat it after meal to boost up their digestion. Ginger is cultivated globally in Africa, the Caribbean, and Asia, where it is used as a cure for nausea. Ginger is as useful and effective as metoclopramide for reducing nausea and emesis. It also treats motion sickness. It is good to use ginger for a person suffering from motion sickness, emesis or nausea because it is inexpensive but readily available and safe to use.

Ginkgo

It is used to treat intracerebral insufficiency. It is one of the existing ancient trees. The Chinese have used it for thousands of years to treat brain disorders. For this reason, Ginkgo is now getting popular worldwide for the same purpose as oxidative damage is prevented by using Ginkgo according to the prescribed methodology. That is why physicians in Germany prescribed a specific method to extract the Ginkgo. In 1997, Ginkgo made a sale of 240 million dollars in the USA. In Germany, Ginkgo has been approved by the official authorities to treat brain circulatory disorders like memory impairment and claudication. In the USA, the Ginkgo was used for the first time to treat dementia in 1997.

Ginseng

It acts as an anticancer and performance enhancer. It is one of the famous and abundantly found herbs in the world. In China, it is taken as a panacea. The old general perception was that it is beneficial for the human body in all aspects. According to the statistical data, almost six million people in the USA use this herb. It works as a tonic for the human body, enhancing the overall metabolism and resistance to stress and promoting vitality as well. In numerous in vitro studies and it has been seen that this herb is effective for endocrine functions and increasing immunity. However, the acceptance ratio varies from human to human.

Goldenseal

Goldenseal is commonly used to treat diarrhea. It is also used as an antiseptic agent. The excess use of this herb can irritate the GI tract, overstimulation of the central nervous system, vasoconstriction, and uterine contractility. Treating oral infections and eye irritations also come under its use. It is an effective and safe remedy to treat the cold as well. Its bioactive agent "Berberine" is an effective, safe, and physio-friendly antidiarrheal agent. Due to the benefits mentioned above, this herb is getting popularity all over the world. But one important precaution which is mandatory to mention here is that goldenseal should not be used by pregnant lady, epileptic patients, cardiac patients and the patients suffering from coagulation problems.

Milk thistle

It is like purple colored flowered plant used for thousands of years to treat liver disorders. Kashmiri people use this plant as a vegetable without having any toxic effect, showing that this plant is safe to eat and can be used as a home remedy. It also prevents the body from "hepatoxic" agents. It resists the toxic effect of various chemical drugs and thus, secures the liver cells from any kind of major damage. No such adverse side effects have been recorded so far. Different countries have allowed its use in encapsulated form with a normal dose of 140 mg per capsule and can be used 2 to 3 times a day.

ST Johns' Wort

This herb is a very good traditional remedy to deal with depression, stress, and hypertension. It is a five-petal flower with yellow color found in wild places worldwide, or we may say that in most of the world. In Europe and the USA, it is highly appreciated at the public level as an antidepressant. However, in Pacific US, its production has reduced as some ranchers think it wills wort a bothersome weed. In Germany, most physicians recommend it to their patients to treat depression as compared to fluoxetine. Between 1995–1997 total sales of this herb, raised 20 times in the USA. Its use as an antidepressant has been approved after various placebo-controlled studies without any side effects, making it safe to use at home.

Saw Palmetto

Fruit extracts of this scrubby palm are historically being used to deal with urogenital problems; even in today's modern time, this herbal treatment is used at the clinical level to enhance the signs of BPH, especially in Europe where it is taken as firsthand treatment with trust without having any kind of significant side effect except mild upset in GI tract and headache. People believe in herbal treatments more than chemically synthesized medicines due to their historical beneficial record, efficacy, and safety. The same is why the Saw Palmetto is getting popular in many developed and underdeveloped countries.

Valerian

It is used as antispasmodic, sleep-aid and anxiolytic. It is a pink-colored flower perennial, abundantly found in the wild areas of high temperature in America and Eurasia. It has been used as a sleep-enhancing agent for centuries. Germany has been approved as a sedative and sleeping aid agent by health officials after seeing its excess use in European countries. In America, it is used as a flavor enhancer in foods and beverages, and no serious harmful effects have been reported. However, a very mild population experienced the paradoxical stimulation, including Palpitations and restlessness due to its long-term use. But Valerian should avoid taking in conjunction with any other sedative, before driving or in the conditions where being alert is necessary.

The physicians must know herbal medications as they are being used for thousands of years. Mostly, the population in Asia, Europe, the USA, and many other countries believe in their safe use. But sometimes, people are misguided due to the lack of knowledge and misconceptions. That is why herbal physicians should know the potential of herbal medication before prescribing it to their patients for treatment.

CHAPTER 3: HERBAL ENCYCLOPEDIA

3.1. Herb's Encyclopedia

There have been unprecedented alterations in herbal medicines since 1996 when the first encyclopedia was published about herbal medication. Herbalism has always been used as a mainstream medication strategy in human history due to its beneficial and healthy effects. That is why this medication strategy is again getting popular in modern developed countries. Today, when people are in the continuous struggle to maintain a healthy and happy lifestyle, the main barrier is continuous depression and stress of earning money and updating the lifestyle in terms of modern accessories. One more factor is pollution and noise. While facing so many problems, people are resistant to using chemical medicines and more intended to herbalism, such as using organic vegetables and different herbs to treat casual mild diseases like BP, headache, sleep disorders and depression. In short, we can say that there is a silent revolution taking place in medical history where the old conventional tricks replace modern hacks to bring soothe and comfort in human life. Researchers are accumulating scientific evidence to prove that herbal medicines are as effective as modern medicines with very mild side effects. Different randomized placebo, controlled studies, and clinical trials are being done to prove the efficacy of herbal medicines. That is why there are numerous pharmaceutical companies all over the world manufacturing herbal medicines under a regularized protocol by government officials.

Herbal Medicines

A variety of herbs having therapeutic characteristics are astonishing. More than 7000 different herbal species varying from small, tiny flowers to trees have been used for medical purposes as home remedies or officially prescribed by physicians. Even today, the Native Americans and Europeans use numerous herbs to deal with health problems.

There are more than 500 herbal plants used in conventional medicines mostly while others are used rarely. For example, there is a plant called Digoxin which was used to treat cardiac diseases in ancient times. But today, a medicine called contraceptive is manufactured from the constituents of Digoxin, proving the claim that herbal medications secure a distinct place in every age of human life due to their unbeatable benefits.

Economic Factors

There are crucial environmental and atmospheric implications related to the use of herbs. For example, growing organic herbs produces opportunities for local farmers and developing countries, especially opportunities for the entire community. We have an example of Brazil where the local population grows different herbs in their small yards and sells them in the market, contributing to the country's net annual revenue and generating employment opportunities for themselves and sometimes for the local population. There is a complete working cycle for herbal products; for example, farmers grow herbs and sell them in the market, where different manufacturing companies purchase them in bulk and produce the herbal items under authorized criteria by the government. These medicines are then distributed to the stores or hospitals where doctors or herbal physicians prescribe them. Even today, in the 21st-century, the majority of the population blindly trusts herbal medicines, instead of allopathic medication, making an inevitable increase in the demand for herbal products in the marketplace. In short, herbal production is a huge market engaging a large population for employment and thus generating considerable economic growth and social development in a country.

How Do the Herbal Plants Work for Medical Purposes?

It is a well-accepted fact that modern medicines play their important part in saving lives and giving relief in extreme conditions. According to an article published in 1993 during the terrible war conditions when doctors ran out of allopathic medicines in hospitals for wound healing in Bosnia, they used an herb called Valerian as a painkiller as well as anesthesia because it is proven from a wide range of medical data history that valerian is effective and useful to treat anxiety and tension. It also works as a sleep enhancer. We emphasize the importance of traditional herbal medicines. Our modern techniques for surgery, for example, plastic surgery and keyhole surgery, and the wide variety of life-supporting machinery available in the market and hospitals, improve the recovery rate from serious injury or disease.

Benefits of Using Herbal Medicines

For the past 70 years, humans are completely relying upon herbal medicines to treat all kinds of illnesses, varying from small problems like colds, headaches, and coughs to larger problems like malaria and tuberculosis. Although medical science has gained a lot of success and popularity, no one can ignore the importance of plant medicines. Again, herbal medicines are getting a keen prominence in the medical world because of their benefits, safety, and efficacy to treat diseases, even serious infections and allergies. Conventional antibiotics, although they are effective in treating serious infections now the viral bacteria have become so habitual to these anti-viral compositions that immediately a new alternative is required, for example, protozoa, an infection causing eukaryote, is no more responsive to the conventional antibiotic treatment.

Sometimes herbal medicines combined with conventional treatment provide a well-defined, tolerating and safeguard remedy for serious chronic diseases. For example, asthma is a kind of bowel syndrome. Treatment of this disease is no more beneficial with the use of biomedicine, and thus, people are now more intending towards a kind of gentle treatment. Thus, we are now in the position to say that people in the western world are now giving space to the ancient tricks of herbal treatment more than modern medicines.

<u>*Use the Herbs but Wisely*</u>

Herbs available abundantly are very safe to use, but it is not true for all the herbs as some plants may cause serious side effects if used consistently and above a defined quantity. There is no doubt that herbal medicines are considered a safe way for treatment. Still, it is quite necessary to use some herbs according to the well-defined guidelines by the physician so that their adverse effects may be avoided. For example, Ma Huang, a famous herb, can be toxic if the patient takes the excess dosage. It may cause severe or sometimes serious liver cell damage, but it rarely happens, especially in those cases where consumption protocols are not followed. Thus, worse effects of herbal medicines can be avoided if they are used carefully. In short, we can say that be careful and remain safe.

<u>*Vigorous plant chemicals*</u>

The extent of affecting the body's mechanism depends upon the chemical composition inside the plant. In the 18th century, scientists started extracting plant chemicals and isolating them for the first time in medical history. Since that time, scientists and researchers have developed a keen interest in looking at the effects of plant medicines, in terms of their chemical composition. This encyclopedia provides detailed information about the major active constituents of herbs, explaining their features and actions.

Isolated herbal constituents are the main concern of research as they are now being used in various worlds' popular and strong medical drugs. For example, the Tubocurarine, which is used as a strong muscle relaxant, is extracted from the Pereira. It is also used as a strong painkiller. Several anesthetics are extracted from the plants and are in wide use in hospitals for surgical purposes and treatment. Even in the 21st century, mostly biomedicines are plants extracted rather than experimented with within the laboratory and equally effective as conventional medicines. There is a pile of literature available proving that most conventional medicines are extracted from the plants.

Importance of whole plants

Although the understanding of each active constituent is necessary but still, herbal products compared to conventional medicines are due to the actions of whole herbal plants. In plants, there are hundreds and thousands of chemical constituents reacting in different complex ways. But still, several herbs are lacking in information that how they work naturally. The whole herb is more important than its constituents, as there are several chemicals inside it reacting in different complex ways to create an effective therapeutic effect. Although it is important to know the active reacting strategy of plants, sometimes this knowledge may be misleading. For example, rhubarb in China is a casually used laxative. It contains "anthraquinones" which irritate the wall of the gut and causes bowel stimulation. This is caused only when this herb is used without following the proper user guide. If taken in a small quantity than the required amount, it may cause dryness in the mucous membrane. Thus, a balanced amount is necessary to be taken for beneficial outcomes. This single example can extract several facts related to the usage of herbal medicines. The 1st of them is that a reliable and comforting relation between a patient and herbal physician can be useful concerning the consumption of herbal products. The 2nd value of an herbal plant is not related to the contents of active constituents. Still, there is an effect of a combined activity.

Herbs as Medicines and Food

It is a historically proven fact that the human body is friendlier with herbal remedies than individually extracted chemical medicines manufactured in different processing plants. The human digestive system is more habitual and friendly towards plant-based foods than junk and processed foods which also secure the medical value. Sometimes it becomes very difficult to draw a line between foods and medicines, especially when we talk about herbal remedies. For example, onions, oats, papayas, and lemons, are taken as food and sometimes together as a medicinal remedy to treat any certain disease. In short, there is the question that whether they are medicines or food. Here is the simple answer that, for example, lemon, effectively treats infections and acts as a strong antioxidant for the human body. Papaya is taken to extract the worms in most parts of the world. Oats are supportive for convalescence. So, we can say that sometimes while talking about herbal medicines, the distinction between medicines and food is removed. This is another surprising fact about herbal medicines.

Respiration, Digestion, and Circulation

For sustaining a good and healthy life, a general trend is to improve the diet first. It is a fact that you are what you eat and somehow it is true because the diet is an essential part of health. If we talk about herbal medicines, they provide the human body with essential nutrients, strengthen the human digestive system, and enhance its metabolic rate. The human body requires a consistent supply of oxygen to perform physical activities, respiration, and food digestion. Herbal food helps the respiratory and lungs system by relaxing the bronchial muscle. Once our body has taken the food, then it is processed by millions of cells. When the body is at rest, then blood flow is mostly towards the center of the body. But in working conditions, our muscles require a continuous supply of oxygen carried out by the blood. Herbal medicines play their key role in stimulating the blood flow and sustaining a continuous metabolic cycle of the human body smoothly.

Clearing the Toxicity and soothing the Skin

The body's waste material should be extracted from the body once nutrients are taken up by the cells. In today's world, much pollution around our body contains many toxic elements because of our polluted environment, poor diet, and ill-health. These toxic elements should be removed from the body to maintain health physically. There are numerous herbal plants available and used by physicians to make the body able to remove the toxic agents immediately out of the body. For example, burdock is a very strong herb to detoxify the body and is used extensively in Chinese and western medicines. Once these harmful elements are removed from the body, our body can then repair the damaged cells and recover much faster than earlier. Skin is also a very important element in maintaining good health, so the herbs like comfrey improve blood clotting and thus helping in the wound healing process.

The Immune and Endocrine System

A healthy nervous system plays an important role in maintaining good health. It is necessary to adapt to the daily demands of life if we want to ensure a healthy and active brain. It is possible only when we do something to avoid anxiety, stress, depression and worries and do sufficient exercise and rest. Brain activity is associated with the endocrine mechanism controlling the releasing of hormones, including the sex hormones affecting vitality and mood. The human's immune system is also linked with the nervous system managing the ability of the human body to resist different infections and fast recovery.

Natural Medicines

We cannot say that herbal medicines are like magic with single-term action. Still, it is a complex natural medicine made up of several active components capable of working on different systems of the human body. Scientific researchers are still going on to know the mechanisms of active constituents of herbal plants.

Active Constituents (Phenols, Flavonoids, Volatile oils & Coumarins)

Phenols are available in varying varieties ranging from aspirin and salicylic acid to complex phenolic glycosides. They are used for anti-inflammatory and antiseptic purposes. Phenolic acids are very strong antioxidants having anti-inflammatory properties. Several mint family members have the properties like phenol, for example, thymol found in thyme.

Flavonoids are very common in the world of plants. These are mostly polyphenolic compounds acting as pigments and usually having yellow or white color. They are very good antioxidants and help in maintaining healthy circulation in the human body. Some have the anti-viral, inflammatory resistant and liver-protecting capability. They have a very important role in strengthening the capillary walls and preventing leakage. Moreover, flavonoids are very effective in treating the symptoms of menopause.

Volatile oils are extracted from herbal plants to get essential oils. They are widely used in perfumery. These are complex mixtures made up of more than 100 compounds. They have a wide range of uses, such as tea oil trees acting as a strong antiseptic. In contrast, gale oil is a strong insect repellent. These oils also have anti-allergic and anti-inflammatory properties useful to deal with infections and allergies.

Coumarins are found in various plant species having divergent actions. Coumarins in horse chestnut and maillot help in keeping the blood in thin concentration. Whereas Bergapten, which is present in the celery plant, helps in tanning the skin, and Khellin, which is found abundantly in "Visnaga," acts as a powerful muscle relaxant.

Proanthocyanins

It is very close to the flavonoids and tannins family. They are mostly in red, blue, and purple color and a very strong antioxidant. They help maintain the body's circulation and protect it from damage, especially in the heart, eyes, feet, and hands. Grapes, red berries, blackberries, all these common fruits contain a considerable amount of these proanthocyanins.

Anthraquinones

These are the main active components found in herbal plants like Senna & Chinese rhubarb. They are very effective in getting rid of constipation. They have a laxative effect on the walls of the large intestine. It stimulates bowel movement. Moreover, it gives the stool a more liquid look making the movement of the bowl easier.

Cardiac Glycosides

It is present in numerous herbal medicinal plants, especially in foxgloves, for example; Digitoxin, Convallotoxin and Digoxin. They are supportive of the heart in maintaining the rate and heart walls' contractions. They are also very diuretic and help in stimulating the production of urine. Cardiac glycosides also help in extracting waste fluid from the tissues and body's circulating system.

Cyanogenic Glycosides

These glycosides contain a considerable amount of cyanide. It is like a potent poison very useful for the relaxant and sedative effect on the muscles and heart. Elder leaves and cherries contain glycosides contributing to the suppressing and soothing ability of plants. Moreover, it gives a very soothing effect if someone is suffering from a dry cough. Glycosides are found abundantly in many fruits like apricot etc.

Polysaccharides

Polysaccharides are composed of multiple units of sugar molecules linked in a certain pattern. According to the research, scientists and herbal physicians, sticky polysaccharides are most important and effective. Generally, they are found in bark, seeds, leaves, and roots. They soak a large quantity of water producing a jelly-like sticky mass beneficial for soothing the irritated tissues like dry skin and inflamed membranes of mucous. These polysaccharides effectively strengthen the human immune system like that of Acemannan, commonly found in Aloe Vera leaves.

Alkaloids

Alkaloids generally contain the nitrogen-bearing ($-NH_2$) molecule, making them active pharmacologically. Some of them are used as well-known drugs and have vast medical use. For example, Vincristine which is derived from Madagascar is used to treat cancer sometimes. Like atropine commonly found in the nightside, many other alkaloids are very beneficial for reducing the body's spasms. Thus, relieving the pain & drying up the body secretions.

Vitamins

Although this fact is neglected, various herbal plants contain a wide range of vitamins for regulating the body's healthy mechanism. Some of them are very common like dog rose to contain a very large concentration of vitamin c Carrots are a very good source of beta carotene. But there are some herbal plants rich in vitamins concentration but are very less common, for example, Watercress having a considerable amount of vitamin B series, E and C and beta carotene

Minerals

Like vegetables and fruits, there are various plants which are a very good source of minerals. Organic plants draw the minerals from the soil and process them to make them in a form easily digestible by the human body. The mineral is like a key factor in the therapeutic activity of any plant, whether taken in the form of vegetables, for example, cabbage, or as medicine like Bladderwrack. Dandelion leaf, which has a high concentration of potassium, is very helpful in repairing the connective tissues and very useful for curing arthritis.

CHAPTER 4: HANDLING OF THE HERBS

4.1. Postharvest Handling of Herbs

Recently various inquiries have been made related to the packaging and postharvest handling of the herbal products to achieve their successful offshore supply and availability in big stores and markets. Before that, there was not significant knowledge available related to the safety, packaging, and efficacy of herbal medicines. As a result, there were a large number of herbal constituents' wastes every year. With their increasing importance, research publications, and clinical trials, there is an utmost effort being put at every level to make the best use of herbal components. However, now the observations related to the careful and wise handling of herbal items Australian herb industry is doing a wonderful job. This industry is contributing with every possible aspect like manufacturing, research, and handling. However, it is necessary to successfully address the problem before taking any measures to resolve it. Keeping this fact in view, it was decided to identify the most common and abundantly used herbs. The industry surveyed to enlist the crops and herbs to secure the top priority. The available literature related to the postharvest and packaging was reviewed before taking the practical measures.

Herbs grown for the retail market or the local wholesale are packed in a variety of ways. The simplest way is to wrap plants' bunches in a polythene sheet to avoid the evaporation of liquid content. But this is not a reliable or authentic way of handling it. Another way to pack the herbs was to take them in bulk and put them into the Styrofoam crate or pack them in waxed cartons. Very few companies exporting herbal products, including oils and medicines, generally use this bulk packaging method.

Local producers have made countless efforts in finding a suitable way to supply the herbs in the market using trial &

error social testing methods. Currently, several ways are being used in the market for the successful and safe supply of herbal products, including plastic sheet bags of consumer size and different plastic sealing methods.

Because of the poor understanding of handling and packaging requirements, there has always been room for improvement at the retail market level. This is why sometimes products like herbs and serums at the retail level are displayed with the temperature above their optimum range. This is one of the major problems being faced in the market related to package handling.

Several distributors are available in the market claim that their packaging technique is best to preserve the quality and freshness of the product. But which method is best is still a question and needs keen research and experiments.

Almost 86% of the distributor and herb growers have no idea about the importance of the packaging. They do not know that how their product is being packed and distributed in the market whether the quality and freshness are sustained or not; whether they are fulfilling the expectation of their purchasers or not. However, some distributors in the market are doing their best to reserve the products' quality via refrigerator supply, where they try to maintain the optimum temperature of the product. Despite using refrigerated vans, there is still the risk of poor handling and poor temperature management, causing warming and quality loss into the market supply chain. With the weak control over temperature requirements and handling protocols quality of the herbal products may be compromised, and thus, wastage is high. There is a common point of concern among all the distributors that while exporting fresh herbs, handling practices, temperature management, and fluctuations during transportation are the major issues that are necessary to be addressed.

Product decaying, moisture loss, and disease development are the major consequences if quality assurance and packaging are not handled properly during the market distribution. 1/3rd of the survey respondents claim that the major problem faced in distributing the fresh herbs was related to the poor postharvest.

Without proper industrial quality standards and an authorized quality assurance system, there is always room for poor products to be supplied in the marketplace, which directly impacts herbal medicines' credibility, safety, and efficacy. That is why good quality material, proper harvest management, well postharvest temperature management and reliable packaging are necessary for a trustworthy medical product. These quality measures are necessary to be taken at every level of the product supply chain, to preserve the credibility and importance of the herbal medicines in the market compared to that of chemically synthesized medicines that already have the advantage of a good package and processing management system.

Quality Control of Herbal Medicines

Large production of herbal medicines is an indication that they are useful and ensures good quality; for example, they are grown properly, dried, and then processed properly under a well-defined protocol authorized by the government health officials. At the same time, working on herbal medicines, ignoring all the safety measures; while talking about herbal medicines, quality is very important. If both the physician and the patient doubt the quality of herbal medicine, it is obviously of no use. That is why quality assurance is the top priority in the case of herbal medicines. Some of the herbal medicines available at the marketplace are very high, but some are very poor, depending upon the government's check and balance policy. According to a survey conducted in the US in 2006, it was reported that only 8 out of 12 herbal products are up to the authorized quality. The quality of herbal items is compromised when there is a deliberate adulteration, and authorities fail to control such factors. There may be some other factors; for example, the crop is poorly harvested, stored, dried, or delayed due to environmental factors. Such herbal products are of no use in which quality is compromised over quantity.

To ensure the best quality herbal product, manufacturers should ensure all the quality control protocols, whether it demands supervision over workers, lab experiments, or other standards. It also includes the routine check and inspection of raw material. This inspection is performed microscopically or with the naked eye. Other quality checks involve ensuring the right concentration of active constituents and other materials.

Purchasing the Herbal Medicine

Dried herbs are usually bought from herbal suppliers. However, purchasing medicines from the shop is more preferred than online shopping, as the purchaser can check the quality from his/her eye at the spot. It does not mean that we should not purchase the product online; some companies supply good quality products for sure. It depends upon their turnover, public remarks and online rating. One should keep in mind that to attain a good effect of medicinal products quality check is compulsory. The person while buying the products should have the following points in his/her mind:

- Herbs are not stored in glass jars or sunlight directly. It may cause unnecessary oxidation affecting their efficacy.

- Herbs have their specific aroma, taste and scent, and they should be sustained.

- Herbs are likely to lose their color with time. The material should be bright and fresh.

While purchasing the herbal processed products like in the form of capsules, oils or tablets, one should always check that he/she is purchasing the labeled products with the following standards:

- All the constituents are mentioned on the label.

- Dosage according to the age is mentioned.

- Volume and weight per capsule or tablet are mentioned.

- The concentration of each component is mentioned.

- The weight of constituents is mentioned.

Herbal Medicines and Big Business

It has been realized by the pharmaceutical companies with major market influence that grasslands, roadsides, fields and rainforests are the major sources of various invaluable medicines. That is why the medical industry has invested a major capital in screening the active constituents in herbal plants worldwide. This research has been very beneficial in producing various herbal products in the plant world. With a patent protocol for synthesizing certain products, a company can make a considerable profit, massive investment for research, and develop new medicines. Herbs are taken as natural remedies. They cannot be patented, only the medicines manufactured under some authorized protocol and certain mechanism containing considerable herbal content. A company can patent a certain herb only when that company specifically finds that herb.

Future of Herbal Medicines

The major issue in the way of herbal medicines is that whether they will be able to secure their traditional knowledge and use. In short, it is necessary to enforce the importance of herbal medicines for their plenty use in the future, and this is somehow happening which is pleasurable. It is necessary to convince people that herbal medicines are not only a valuable substitute for chemically processed medicines but a very good and effective way of treatment for various infectious, viral, and allergic diseases. For several decades, courses are being studied in Indian and Chinese educational institutes; however, this process is comparatively slower in the West. Western countries are also paying valuable importance to herbal products and accepting their significance for the past two decades, especially in Germany, UK, the USA, and Australia. Herbal therapy has become part of their medical syllabus. Medical students have the choice to select between herbalism and other subjects. This is happening just because, since ancient times, herbal medicines have always been a very staunch part of the medical world. It seems that shortly, patients will have the choice to choose between herbal treatment or the other way of cure depends which therapy best suits them.

CHAPTER 5:
HERBS AND MODERN MEDICINES

5.1 Native American Herbs and Modern Health Supplements

Native Americans are famous for their knowledge about herbalism. It is believed that Americans are the first to use plants and herbs for medical purposes. Native Americans are thought to have a spiritual view of the plants. Many modern herbal remedies are based on the ancient knowledge of Americans. The most commonly used plants for medical are enlisted below:

Yarrow

It is a fragrant plant. In ancient times Greeks used this plant to stop excess bleeding and wound healing purposes. They also mix the juice of the yarrow flower with water to cure the upset stomach and deal with the disorder in the digestive system. Its' stems and leaves were used to make tea acting as astringent.

Rosemary

This plant was considered sacred by the Native Americans. It was used mostly to deal with the joints' sore. It is an excellent memory enhancer, a very good relief for spasm and muscle pain, and maintains the nervous system and body's circulation system. It also gives strength to the digestive and immune systems.

Mint

Mint is a very good antioxidant and abundantly used herb by Native Americans since ancient times. It also cures the upset stomach and gives relief from the skin rashes and itching.

Red Clover

This plant is used to treat respiratory disorders and inflammation. It also helps in treating heart diseases and hyperlipidemia.

Black Gum Bark

Black gum bark has been used to treat chest pains since ancient times. It is also used in food, crafts and medicines. Moreover, Cherokee people used to make tea from this.

Greenbrier

This plant has been used as a pureblood and pain killer since ancient times. Its leaves were used to make slaves and mixed with the hog lard useful for burns, sores, and scalds.

Hummingbird Blossom

The Native Americans used this flowery plant to treat throat and mouth conditions, cysts, inflammations, and fibroid tumors. It also helps in relieving form wounds, burns and sores. Its roots are used to make the diuretic stimulating kidney function. It was also used to make black tea by the ancient people. Recent research studies have revealed the fact that this plant is effective for lowering high blood pressure.

Saw Palmetto

Native tribes in Florida used this plant as food, but herbal physicians used it to make a natural remedy to treat abdominal pain. It is also very useful for stimulating appetite and reducing inflammation. It also helps indigestion.

Sage

This plant is generally used to make spices. But in ancient times, it was considered as the sacred plant by the native tribes of America. They thought this plant has spiritual purifying energies, which extracts their negative energies and cleanse their souls. But this plant has many medical uses, like treating colds, cramps, flu, and bruises. It is also used to deal with abdominal pain.

Wild Ginger

In the herbal world, this plant has been used to treat ear infections. Its rootstocks were used to make mild tea, an effective stimulating agent for digestion. This plant is also very useful to treat nausea and bronchial infections.

Lavender

Herbal physicians used to make a natural remedy using this plant to treat insomnia, fatigue, depression, anxiety, and headache. Oil made from this plant has antiseptic and anti-inflammatory properties. Its oil is also used in fusion with other herbal oil to treat burns and insect bites.

Honeysuckle

Native Americans used this plant to treat asthma, but this is still used for multi healing purposes, for example, for arthritis, hepatitis, and mumps. It is also very beneficial to cure infections in the upper respiratory tract.

<u>**Mullein**</u>

It is like the tobacco plant used commonly to treat respiratory disorders. Its roots were used to make concoctions by the Native Americans having healing properties for swelling in the feet, hands, and joints.

<u>**Devils' claw**</u>

Although it seems to be a poisonous plant by the name, it was used to treat various health disorders by the Native Americans, from skin infections to fever. It is also very useful for digestion and arthritis. Tea made from this plant is effective in dealing with diabetes. Moreover, this natural herbal remedy is also used to reduce swelling, joint pains, back pain, sores and headache.

5.2. Native American's medical system

The traditional healing system of Native Americans is recognized by the NCCAM-National Center for Complementary & Alternative Medicine as an indigenous way of treating various diseases' acute & chronic conditions. However, tribal differences in term of healing remedies exist on the individual level but still shares interventional strategies and health beliefs regarding socio-bio-psycho traditional and spiritual approaches. Native Americans of Arizona use to run every day to greet dawn for the spiritual wellbeing. Still, manipulative therapies of herbs, prayers, and ceremonies are practices to treat and prevent the diseases. Traditional indigenous healing systems have been used for thousands of years for the well-being and healthy lives of the Native Americans with encouraging successful outcomes. The locals still practice these ancient hacks in various parts of America to meet the health demands. But today, with the demands of developing time, ancient healing traditions are being infused with the modern medical world to promote the wellbeing of health conditions.

Along with the old native hacks, spiritual healing tricks are also considered an integral part of American native culture. However, there exists a conflict among modern medical physicians on the matter of spiritual healing hacks. They take it as an irritating and uncomfortable way of treating with no significant results. They are introducing new and modern methods of medical practices instead of old and traditional socio-spiritual tricks. But it is the reality that we cannot ignore the importance of ancient spiritual and natural remedies, which have successfully healing different severe health conditions in the medical world for thousands of years.

CONCLUSION

Herbal medicines have been an integral part of the medical world for thousands of years. People believe in herbal remedies and use herbal products to meet their healthcare needs; developing countries like Germany, UK, the USA, and Europe are taking essential measures to incorporate ancient natural tricks, into the modern medical system considering the importance of herbalism socially. National health authorities are working to ensure the safety, quality, and efficacy of herbal products. Since the last few decades, considerable research and clinical trials have been done, proving the effectiveness of herbal products to treat several diseases from mild status to chronic. That is why now, in various developed countries, authorities are working on the regularization of herbal products. Since 1996, there have been unprecedented alterations in herbal medicines since when 1st herbal encyclopedia was published. In human history, herbalism has always been the mainstream strategy to deal with different health conditions. Stress and depression of getting a better lifestyle is the biggest barrier in the way of healthy life. To deal with this issue, herbal medicines are the best solution with natural treatment giving an easy, feasible, economical and long-lasting healthy impact physically and psychologically. Briefly, there is a silent revolution taking place in the medical world in terms of herbalism.

www.ingramcontent.com/pod-product-compliance
Lightning Source LLC
Chambersburg PA
CBHW070745030726
47601CB00001B/157